Rachel Burke.

# 30 Irish Tunes *for* EASY RECORDER

GW00538379

## by Ellen Cranitch

# CONTENTS

ISBN - 1 85720 091 8

Copyright © 1987 Walton Manufacturing Ltd.
Unit 6A, Rosemount Park Drive, Rosemount Business Park, Ballycoolin Road, Blanchardstown, Dublin 15, Ireland.

*U.S. Distributors*: Walton Music Inc., P.O. Box 874, New York, NY 10009, U.S.A.

# Fingering Chart
# for Descant Recorder

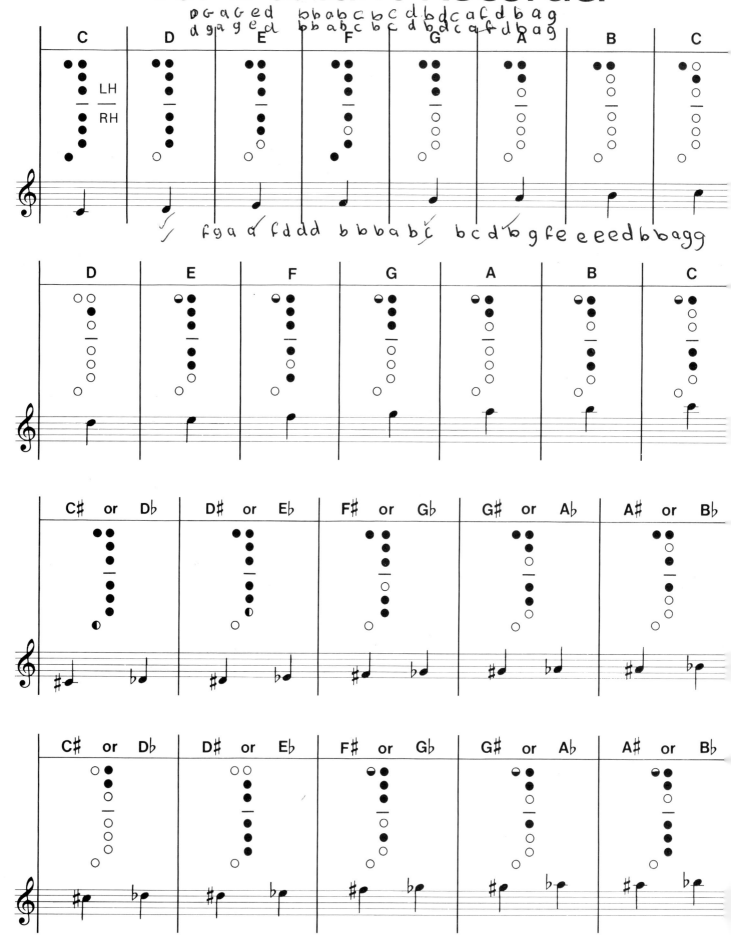

# Oft In The Stilly Night

# The Minstrel Boy

# I Know My Love

# The Rakes Of Mallow

4

# Anach Cuain

# The Foggy Dew

5

# Óró Sé Do Bheatha Bhaile

# The Galway Shawl

# The Cliffs Of Doneen

# Nora

# The Lark In The Clear Air

# Love Is Teasin'

# Sí Beag Sí Mór

# Beir Mé Ó

# The Dawning Of The Day

# Cockles And Mussels

# The Curragh Of Kildare

# Planxty Irwin

# Tabhair Dom Do Lámh

# The Star Of The County Down

# The Coulin

# Down By The Glenside

# Brian Boru's March

# Táimse im Chodladh

# I Know Where I'm Going

# Carolan's Draught

# The Sally Gardens

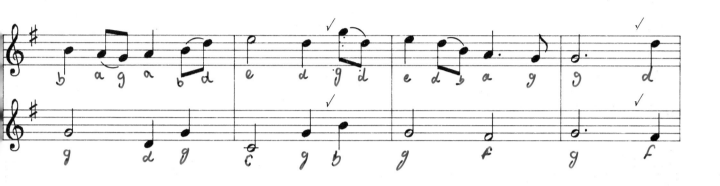

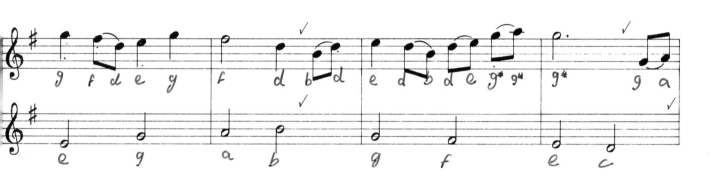

# The Last Rose Of Summer

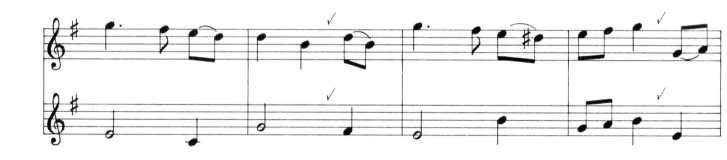

# The Connemara Cradle Song

# The Spinning Wheel